Asp.Net For Beginners

The Simple Guide to Learning Asp.Net Web Programming Fast!

Table Of Contents

Introduction

I want to thank you and congratulate you for downloading the book Asp.Net for Beginners.

This book contains proven steps and strategies on how to become a truly skilled and talented Asp.Net user. It will take you from the very basics of this programming method, to in depth views and examples of what it can do and what it has to offer you. If you are ready to learn how to apply the techniques of Asp.Net to your website or other online sites, then you have found the ideal guide to get started.

You will need some time to become efficient with this programming language; however, when you learn the basics, which is what is taught here, you will find that learning the more advanced skills is much easier.
The step by step information in this book takes you through what Asp.Net is, how it works, and why you should use it. This is truly your one-stop-shop to getting started with Asp.Net.

It's time for you to become an amazing Asp.Net developer and learn to use this programming language to its full potential. Let's get started!

Chapter 1: What is Asp.Net?

Are you ready to get started with Asp.Net? If so, you should first understand what it is and what it is capable of doing. This is a type of platform for web development where you will find an easy-to-use programming model, complete software infrastructure, as well as a number of other services that are necessary to create versatile web applications for PCs and mobile devices.

It is considered an open source and server-side Web application framework that is designed for those in web development to create various dynamic web pages. Originally developed by programmers at Microsoft for building web services, web applications, and web sites, it is now an easy-to-use option that many people new to programming languages turn to.

This platform will work over the traditional protocol for HTTP and it will use the HTTP policies and commands in order to create a direct correlation between the browser and server as a type of bilateral cooperation and communication.

It is also considered part of the Microsoft .Net well-known platform. Its applications include complied codes, which are written with the reusable and extensible objects or components that are present in the .Net framework. It is these codes that are able to use the whole hierarchy of different classes found in the framework of .Net.

The application codes for Asp.Net are able to be used along with any of these languages:

- J#
- Jscript
- Visual Basic.Net
- C#

The programming model is also able to be used for producing data driven and interactive web applications that are used with the internet. Asp.Net includes a number of different controls, including buttons, text boxes, and various labels for the manipulation, configuration and assembly of code in order to create the actual HTML pages.

The Asp.Net Model for Web Forms

The web forms created with Asp. Net are used for extending the activity driven model regarding integration of the various web applications. Part of the process involves the browser submitting the web form over to the actual web server, then the server returning a complete HTML page or markup page as a response.

Since HTTP is considered to be a protocol that is stateless, the framework of Asp.Net will help to store the various information in regard to the application state, consisting of:

- Session state
- Page state

Page state refers to the client's state, for example, the content that is in different input fields on the created web form. Session state refers to all of the information that is obtained from the different pages that the user not only visited, but also worked with, for example the complete session state. In order to fully understand this concept, consider this example of how it works with a traditional shopping cart.

When a user adds something to the shopping cart, these items are added from a certain page. This is referred to as the products page, and then the total items that are collected, in addition to the price are displayed on another page, referred to as the shopping cart page. However, HTTP is not capable of keeping up with all the different information that is being sent from various pages. The session state Asp.Net, as well as the infrastructure of the server side will help to keep the entirety of the information organized during the user's session.

The runtime of Asp.Net will carry the page state back and forth to the server as well as across all the page requests all while it is generating various runtime codes. These are then incorporated in the state on the server side in the hidden fields that are present.

This ensures that the server remains alert of the application state and that it operates in a way that is connected.

The Component Model for Asp.Net

This is considered as an object model – put simply it provides a number of building blocks for Asp.Net pages. This works to describe:

- Virtually all the HTML elements or tags, including <input> and <form>.
- The server controls that will help in developing the complicated user-interface. An example of this would be the Gridview control or Calendar control.

Asp.Net is considered a type of technology that works with the entire .Net framework and that contains all of the different web functionalities. Also, the framework of .Net is created from a hierarchy that is object-oriented. The web application for Asp.Net is created from pages. In instances when the user requests the Asp.Net page, then the IIS will delegate the page processing to the runtime system of Asp.Net.

The runtime of Asp.Net will then transform the used .aspx page to instances of a certain class that will be inherited from the foundation of the actual .Net framework to the class page. This means that each of the Asp.Net pages is considered to be an object and each of the components, or the controls on the server side, are also considered objects.

The .Net Framework Components

Before you go on with the next area of learning Asp.Net, it is essential that you fully understand all of the different components in terms of the actual .Net framework. The following list will provide you with all the components that you will encounter as you work with the platform:

CLR or Common Language Runtime

This performs compilation, verification, code safety, code execution, thread execution, security checking, debugging, exception handling, and memory management. The code that is created is managed directly by the actual CLR and referred to as managed code. After it has been compiled, the compiler will convert the actual source code to the CPU IL, or independent intermediate language code. Then the Just in Time (JIT) compiler will turn the IL code into the required native code that is specific for each CPU.

LINQ

This works to impart the data querying ability to .Net languages by using a syntax that is very similar to the usual language of SQL.

Windows CardSpace

Offers a safety for being able to access resources and to share personal information while on the internet.

WCF or Windows Communication Foundation

This is the actual technology that is used for building and then executing various connected systems.

Windows Presentation Foundation

This offers separation in between the business logic and user interface. When used properly, it can aid in creating interfaces that are visually stunning by implementing media, documents and several animations, dimensional graphics and other elements.

WF or Windows Workflow Foundation

This will help in the creation of any workflow-based application used in Windows. It will contain a number of activities, workflow designer, workflow runtime, and a rules engine.

Ado.Net

Refers to the technology that is used for working with various types of data and different databases. It offers you access to a number of data sources, such as the SQL server, OLE DB XML and more. It will also provide a connection to various data sources to use for updating, manipulating, and retrieving data.

Asp.Net

Refers to the actual model of web development and the term Asp.Net AJAX is also common, which is referring to an extension of the Asp. Net, which will allow you to implement the AJAX functionality. It contains the various components that allow the developer to be able to update the data that is located on your website, getting rid of the need to completely reload the current page.

Windows Forms

This offers a graphical representation of the various windows that are displayed in the actual application.

Assemblies and Metadata

The term metadata is the various binary information that describes a program, which will be either stored in some type of portable executable file, or PE, or in the actual memory. The assembly is going to be a logical unit that consists of the IL code, type metadata, assembly manifest and a number of set resources, for example, image files.

Common Type System

This offers various guidelines for managing, using, and declaring various types of runtime and the cross-language communication.

Common Language Specification

This is what includes the various specifications for the actual .Net supported languages and the actual implementation of the language integration.

Advantages Offered by Asp.Net

When compared to other web development methods, Asp.Net offers a number of advantages, which include:

- Reduces the total amount of code that is needed to build larger applications.
- Peace of mind that your applications are secured and save with the built-in Windows pre-application configuration and authentication.
- Provisions of higher quality performance by using early binding, native optimization, just in time compilation, and services that are right out of the box.

- Framework is able to be complemented with a full toolbox and a designer in the using Visual Studio integrated environment. Offers automatic deployment, drag and drop controls, and WYSIWYG editing as a few of the features that are offered by Asp.Net.
- Complete simplicity in terms of performing common tasks from the simple submission of forms, deployment, authentication for clients, and overall site configuration.
- Easy to write and maintain since the Asp.Net pages and the HTML source code are together.
- Close management and monitoring by the Asp.Net runtime.
- Can easily work with Ado.Net in terms of data binding and features of page formatting.
- Continual monitoring by the Web server of the applications and components running on the actual page.

Put simply, Asp.Net is the next generation in the Microsoft ASP. It provides a framework for programming that can be used for creating technologies, web applications, and enterprise class websites. When Asp.Net developed applications are used, they can be accessed on a global basis and lead to more efficient information management. No matter if you are working to build a huge corporate web application or a small business website, Asp.Net offers a viable programming platform that allows the work to get done as quickly as possible.

Chapter 2: Getting Started with Asp.Net

When you are ready to get started and fully understand what Asp.Net is and what it can do, you will need to acquire and install a copy of the Microsoft Visual Web Developer. While you do not have to have this to use Asp.Net, it is a good idea. However, if you would rather, you can utilize Notepad. Keep in mind, however, VWD was created for the sole purpose of creating Asp.Net web sites and web applications.

Getting VWD

The good news is that it is quite easy to acquire your own copy of VWD. There is a free version available on the Microsoft site, which means you can get started with Asp.Net at no charge to you. You can also choose the full version, but it will cost a bit more; however, the additional features, tools, and programs make it worthwhile.

Once you have successfully installed VWD, you are ready to start creating your very first Asp.Net website!

Diving In: Your First Asp.Net Website

Chances are you are eager to get started with your very first Asp.Net website. Instead of getting a technical overview of VWD here, we will get right to the action and explain how you can create your very first project.

The first step is to start your VWD program – which ever version you decided to download. Once you start it, you will have to configure the new program; however, there will be a step by step process that takes you through this. After the configuration process is complete, you will see the main screen for the application appear.

At this point you should simply focus on creating your very first website. In order to do this, click the button "File" in the left, upper corner and then select "New website." In the installed templates section that will be on the left of your screen, you can choose the programming language that you are planning to use for your website. You should verify that Asp.Net is chosen. Also, verify that the File System is the chosen option in the drop down list at the bottom left corner. Once you have done this, you click "OK," and VWD will create your new website that includes several folders and files to help and jump start the process.

When you click "OK" you will also see the Default.aspx file opened, where you can see the page code.

In order to change the text on the web page, you will have to use code. For example:

```
<asp:Content ID="BodyContent" runat="server"
ContentPlaceHolderID="MainContent">
```

```
<h2>Hi there</h2>
```

```
<p>Getting started with Asp.Net on
<%DateTime.now.ToSring() %></p></asp:Content>
```

Once you have inserted the code you will see the text you have put in the code brackets. Press the Ctrl+F5 in order to open this page in the web browser you are using. When it opens you will see the text you have created.

If you see a dialog box that is requesting you to sign in, you will have to close the browser and return to VWD. Here you will right click the site that is found in Solution Explorer and select "Property Pages." When you reach the Smart options section, simply clear away the check in the box that reads "NTLM Authentication item." Once you do this, you can click OK and then Ctrl + F5 again in order to view the page that you have created in your actual web browser.

During your development process, VWD will continue to provide you with "tips" to help you along your way.

Essentially, that is all there is to creating your very first web page.

It is important that you take note that the actual ASPX file that you modified with VWD will not be the one that is displayed in your web browser. When you have created a page with VWD, you will add some markup to it. When talking about an ASPX page, the markup refers to any combo of HTML, code and plain text for the Asp.Net server controls.

If you request the ASPX page in your actual web browser, then the web server will actually process the page and then execute any instances of code that are found in the file, helping to transform the markup in Asp.Net into the plain HTML language. This will then send it to the actual web browser where it is going to be displayed.

More about Using Asp.Net

If you were to type in any web address in your browser and hit enter, then the browser is going to send this request to the web server at the address. The process is done with HTTP, which is the HyperText Transfer Protocol. This is the protocol that web servers and web browsers use to communicate. After you type in a certain address, there will be a request sent to the actual server. When it is an accurate request, you will be displayed the requested page.

Since you are going to be using the Development Web Server that is built in, essentially the client and server are the exact same machine. However, in actual scenarios, you will be hosting the website on a third party hosting service so that it can be accessed by a number of different clients.

For the simple files that are also static, such as images or HTML files, the server will just read the file from the hard drive and then send it over to the browser. However, in the case of the dynamic files – AspX pages – you know this will not be good enough. If the ASPX file was sent right to the web server as a text file, then you would not actually see the current time or date in the browser, but rather see the code that you have inserted.

Rather than having the file directly sent, the server will be handing the request over to a different piece of software that will be used for processing the page. The Handler Mapping or Application Mapping is what is used to ensure the file being sent is able to be handled. When it comes to the .aspx page, the request will be processed at the Asp.Net runtime, which had been specifically designed for handling requests from the web.

While the page is being processed, there are three primary areas that can influence the way that the page is ultimately seen in a web browser:

- Static Test: This will be sent to the browser as is and includes JavaScript, CSS and HTML.
- Asp.Net Server Controls: Found in the ASPX page and when processed they will emit the HTML that is then inserted into the actual page.
- Programming Code: When you embed code such as C#, Visual Basic.Net on your page then you will place it in the Code behind file. This is then executed by the actual user's action or by the runtime.

After the processing of the page is complete and the HTML has been completely collected, then the actual HTML is resent to the browser. This is when the browser will read, parse, and then display the page that you see.

If you are familiar with HTML, you will have a head start with Asp.Net. If not, you should take some time to become familiar with the basics of HTML.

Markup of Asp.Net

Asp.Net Server Controls markup is extremely similar to HTML. It uses the notions of attributes, elements and tags all using the same type of angle brackets, as well as the closing tags that HTML uses. However, there are also a number of differences that are present.

One of the main differences is that the majority of Asp.Net tags are going to begin with asp: as a prefix. The button for Asp.Net will look like this:

```
<asp:Button ID="Button1" runat="server" Text+"Click Me" />
```

You should take note that the tag is then self-closed with the slash (/) that is trailing a character, which will eliminate the necessity of typing a different closing tag.

Another primary difference is that the attribute and tag names are not always in lowercase format. Since the Asp.Net server control actually lives on the server, it does not necessarily adhere to the rules for XHTML that are used in the client's browser. When the Server Control has been asked to emit the HTML to the page that has been configured for outputting XHTML it will do it in a way so that the button code looks like this when it is placed in the browser as actual XHTML:

```
<input type="submit" name="Button1" value="Click Me"
id="Button1" />
```

The attributes and tag have conformed to the standard
XHTML.

Helpful Tips for Using the Visual Web Developer

When you are using the VWD there are a number of tips that
can help you make it more functional. One thing you should
do is to play around with the VWD platform in order to see
what it offers. Try to add a few pages to the site and then use
the drag and drop feature from the Toolbox onto the pages
and then view them in the browser. This will allow you to
have a much better understanding of the controls and the
tools that are available for you to use. When you browse
through all of the settings you will be able to learn how to
tweak other features of the design to ensure your site offers
everything you want it to.

Chapter 3: Website Building with Asp.Net

While the previous chapter gave you a general overview of using VWD, you need a bit more in depth knowledge to make a truly impressive website. There is much more to creating a website than the few steps previously outlined. For example, you can choose from templates, tools and features that have not yet been covered. Now is time to explore these in more detail.

Creating Your Website Project

Creating a VWD website begins by finding the Website projects option. Here you will create a new project by:

- Selecting File
- File or New Website
- New
- Website from the VWD's primary menu

Web Applications Projects

When you opt for Web Applications Projects, it will be easier for teams of developers to work together in order to create the site you really want.

Selecting a Template

You will find a number of template options available in the New Web Site dialog box found in VWD.

In the left hand portion, you will be able to select from Visual C# and visual basic as the site's programming language. The middle section displays the default Asp.Net templates. If you get to the point where you can create your own templates, they will show up in this location, as well.

The Website of Asp.Net

A good starting point when selecting a template for your website is the Empty website template. This will provide you with a single configuration file. This will be extremely useful if you have quite a few current files that you are planning to use for creating a new website or if you are trying to develop the site completely from scratch. You can use this template as the entire basis for a website that you create, and then add the folders and the files as you continue working through the process.

WCF Service

This is the template that allows you to create websites that offer more than a single WCF service. This is similar to a web service in the regard that it will allow you to create methods that are able to be called over a network.

Websites with Dynamic Data

There are two templates which are available for Dynamic Data and that will allow you to make a flexible, but powerful site where you can manage data in your database without having to use very much manual code.

Creating then Opening Your New Website

There are several different methods that you can use for creating a new website or opening a new one. The options that you have will be largely influenced by the way that you access the website and if you are going to use the included web server that goes along with VWD or the one that is available through Windows.

Creating a Brand New Website

The first step required for creating a new Asp.Net website is to create a folder that is called BegASPNET in the C drive root by using My Computer or Windows Explorer. In the folder you should create another folder that you name "site." This will result in a folder that is called C:\BegASPNET\Site.

Once the folder has been created, you should start the Visual Web Developer and then choose:

- File
- New website or file
- New project

Once you arrive you will choose between either Visual C# or Visual Basic. In the area that is in the middle, you should choose Asp.Net "Empty Website." You should also make sure that the file system is chosen in the Web Location list. The other options – FTP and HTTP – will allow you to open a site that is running IIS with the FrontPage program.

Once selected, choose the Browse button that is next to the text box and browse to the created folder that you made a few steps ago and select "open."

Once you have found the folder, click OK and the new site will be created for you by VWD.

Since you are creating a website that is based on the Empty Web Site template, it is still just a simple folder in Windows that VWD is looking at.

Opening an Existing Website

Much like creating a brand new website, when you open an existing site with VWD, you will be presented a few options in regard to the source location of the actual website. You will have the option to open the site from a remote site, using FTP, from the local IIS web server or even a local file system.

The site that you are creating is definitely bare bones and in order to make it more useful you will have to add additional files in it.

Working with the Website Files

The Asp.Net website will consist of, at minimum, one Web Form, which is the file with the .aspx extension; however, in most cases it will consist of more files. There are a number of different file types available with VWD, with each one offering a specific functionality.

Types of Files for Asp.Net Websites

The various file types available are listed here and you can create categories to keep them organized. The most important files that you will create are found here.

Web Files

These are specific to various web applications and can be requested directly by a browser or can be sued to build up a portion of the web a page that the browser has requested. The following lists the web files, as well as their extensions and offers a description of how each file is going to be used.

- Web Form: .aspx – this is the workhorse of the Asp.Net website.
- Master Page: .master – Allows you to define the structure, feel and look for your website.

- Web User Control: .ascx – includes page fragments that are able to be reused in different pages on your website.
- Skin File: .skin – Offers information for the controls of your website.
- Jscript File: .js – Includes JavaScript that is able to be executed by the browser of the client.
- Site Map: .sitemap – This offers a hierarchical representation of all the files on your site in XML format.
- Web Configuration File: .config – Site wide information contained here.
- Style Sheet: .css – Contains the CSS code that will allow you to format and style your website.
- HTML Page: .html/.htm – Used for displaying the static HTML on your website.

Code Files

The way you add code files to your website is exactly the same as how you add the web files. Some of the different types of code files include:

- .ASAX – Globalb App. Class: Contains code that is presented in a response to anything interesting that occurs on the site.
- .CS/.VB – Class: Contains the cold that will be used for programming your website.
- .ASMX – Web Service: Contains code that is able to be executed through your server.

Data Files

These files are used for storing data that is able to be used on your website, as well as other applications. This category of files includes files that are related to working with data, database files and XML files. The specific files included here are:

- .DBML – Ado.Net: Used for accessing databases declaratively eliminating the need to write any code.
- .MDF – SQL: these are files that are sued by the Microsoft SQL server.
- .XML – XML Files: Used for storing data in the XML format.

Adding Your Existing Files

When you create files for your website, not all of them have to be completely new. In a number of cases, it will make sense for you to reuse files you have from other projects. You may be able to reuse your CSS file across a number of sites, or even a logo. Adding existing files is actually quite easy. Simply right click your website in the Solution Explorer and then choose the "Add Existing Item" option. When the dialog box pops up, you can look through the files to find what you are looking for. You can select multiple ones if necessary. When you have selected all of the files you want to add, you can simply click "Add."

Organizing Your Website

Due to the large number of files that are going to be on your site, it is usually a good idea to make groups them by their function, all in individual folders. For example, put all of your Style Sheet files in a folder that is called Styles.

Special Types of Files

There are a number of files that are listed above that you can place in a special folder, rather than the organizational folder structure that was listed earlier.

Working with the Web Forms

The web forms that you create are going to be represented by the .aspx files, which is at the very foundation of any Asp.Net web application. These are going to be the pages that people visiting your site are going to see.

Using VWD will allow you to look at the web form from a number of different angles. The fact is that VWD allows you to view your pages and try to create the website that you really want.

Chapter 4: Security when Using Asp.Net for Your Website

When you are using Asp.Net web applications a crucial aspect of this is security. Here you will learn background information regarding various security issues that may come up when using web applications, how to mitigate the most common security risks, how to protect the application resources and how you can authorize and authenticate different users.

If an unknown user is able to access the Web application you are working on, there is a good chance that a malicious user will attempt to get unauthorized access to the application, as well. If you have servers accessible to the general public online, then they are being probed constantly for vulnerabilities. This is why it is highly recommended that you take certain precautions to ensure security is built into all of the web applications you develop.

Solution Part One: Security Technology

One part of the solution is implementing security measures. Another important aspect is being vigilant. Even if you have a system with a number of different safeguards, you have to watch it very closely in the following ways:

- Keep track of the event logs of your systems. Be sure that you are aware of any attempts of someone trying to log on to your system or if there are multiple requests that are being made against the web server.

- Be sure that your application server is updated with the latest in security updates to ensure that your website remains safe.

Threat Modeling

One of the most important parts of developing a solution that is more secure is to understand the various threats that are present. The good news is that Microsoft has worked to create a way to categorize the various threats that are present. These are found here.

Spoofing

The word spoof is when someone is trying to impersonate a process or user in order to gain access in an unauthorized manner. Put simply, a spoofer is a malicious attempt to gain access to your website and data.

Generally speaking, you can minimize the chance of spoofing when you use a stringent type of authentication. At any point that someone attempts to access information that is anything but public, be sure that they are actually who they say they are. Another way to protect yourself from spoofing is by ensuring that your credential information is going to remain safe. This means that you should not keep your passwords or any other sensitive information located in a cookie, where there may be a malicious user trying to modify it.

Tampering

This refer to deleting or changing a resource when authorization has not been granted. An example of this would be defacing a certain web page, where the malicious user is able to access your site and change the files. One of the most popular indirect methods of eliminating the change of tampering is to use script exploit. In most cases, malicious users will manage to get a script to begin to execute when it is masked as the user input from one of your pages or a link.

The main source of defence in regard to tampering is to use the security provided by Windows in order to lock down your Windows resources, directories and files.

Repudiation

This type of threat involves a transaction that leaves no proof it was eve present. In regard to a web application this may mean impersonating the credentials of an innocent user. You may be able to protect yourself form repudiation if you use stringent authentication. You should also use the Windows logging features in order to keep a trail of any other activity that takes place on the server.

Information Disclosure

This refers to simply revealing or stealing information that should remain private. One of the most common examples of this would be stealing passwords; however information disclosure may also involve access to any resource of file that is on the server.

The best way to protect yourself against information disclosure is to ensure that there is no information to disclose. This means that you avoid the storage of your passwords, so that malicious users will not be able to steal them.

Denial of Service

This type of attack is to deliberately cause one of the applications to no longer be available. One example of this would be a Web application overload. Malicious users may also attempt to crash your server.

Elevation of Privilege

This type of attack involves attempting to gain more permission than what is usually assigned.

Using Asp.Net and Storing Sensitive Information

When you are using Asp.Net for your website, it may require you to use quite a bit of sensitive information. An example of this would be using a user identification and password for connecting to a database, or if you are storing any customer's passwords and IDs. There is the option to use SSL or secure sockets layer for encrypting the information when it goes over the network, the information will also have to be protected in some way when it is stored on your server and on the actual client.

Avoid the Storage of Sensitive Info

One of the best ways that you can avoid the exposure of any sensitive information in your Asp.Net application is just not to store it to begin with. Try to avoid putting any information in a cookie or into a control that is found in the browser.

Encrypt all Sensitive Information

If you are storing sensitive information, you should not store it in any human-readable text or in a format that is easy to decode. This will ensure that it is highly protected.

Asp.Net and Limiting Access to Your Websites

There are two topics to consider when you are working to limit access to an application:

- Authentication: This is how a certain application identifies who a person is.
- Authorization: Is the way that the application determines what you are allowed to do.

Authenticating Your Users

With Asp.Net you have a number of different options when it comes to authenticating users. If you have a read-online application that is able to be viewed by anyone, you should use anonymous authentication. If you want to ensure more restricted access to the application, you should use a form that is designed to identify the users. There are two basic identities that you need to consider when you are authenticating users for the Asp.Net application:

- User identity for Asp.Net that is used for identifying a user for Asp.Net
- The application identity which is used for accessing the Windows resources

While your application is able to run without the user identity with Asp.Net, you will still have the Windows application identity. In order to help and secure your application further, you need to restrict the actual Windows identity for the application in question, including the database and file access.

Application Identity for Asp.Net

When one of your Asp.Net pages is executing, then the server has to have security context, or an identity for the process that is actually executing the code in question. This identity will then be used when you are securing resources such as the network, NTFS file system or regular files.

The actual identity of the Asp.Net application will be determined by a number of different factors. As a default option, the pages made with Asp.Net will run with the Windows identity of the processes and service on the Asp.Net pages.

The User of Asp.Net

This is a person who is able to access specific resources. You can identify a part of the application that is available to certain users, while other parts are available to all of the users.

The user qualifications are determined by the process of authentication of the system.web, which is found in the Wed.config file for the application. There are a number of different options available for authenticating the identity for your specific application. You can use the actual Windows user name that has been given by the ISS, use Passport authentication, use Asp.Net forms authentication or even your own, unique authentication scheme.

Authorizing the Users

When you are authorizing a user, it will involve restricting access to the resources that are necessary. This will include restricting access to only the needed files, the databases or the other portions of your particular application. Additionally, this will include using a type of code access security in order to restrict the actual access code.

Chapter 5: Cookies and Asp.Net

When cookies are used on a site, they allow the Web applications to store information about those who visit the website. An example of this would be storing a user's preferences when they visit your site. If the user then visits your same website at another time, then the application will be able to access this previously stored information to use and enhance the user experience.

The Background of Cookies

Cookies are tiny bits of text, which will accompany the pages and requests as they move in between the actual web server to the browser. Cookies contain information that the actual Web application will be able to read if the user comes to the website.

This means that if a visitor to the site requests a certain page from the website and the application sends the page, along with a cookie that contains the time and date, when the page arrives at the user's browser, it will also get the cookie. This is then stored in a pre-determined folder that is on the hard drive of the user's computer.

Down the road, if the same user requests any page that is on your website again, when the URL is entered, the browser will take a look at the hard drive for the cookie that is related to the actual URL. If there is a cookie present, then the browser will send this cookie to the website in addition to the actual page request. The application will then be able to determine the last time and date that the visitor was there. You may also utilize the information for displaying messages aimed at your visitor in order to check a certain expiration date.

It is important to remember that cookies are directly related to your actual website, rather than a single page. This means that the server and browser is going to exchange information about cookies no matter the page that is requested.

Cookies help various websites to store information about their visitors. Generally, cookies provide a way to continually maintain your web application. Besides the brief period of time when information is being exchanged, the web server and browser will be disconnected. Each of the requests that a user makes to your server ac always treated as an independent action of any other request that is being made. In many cases, however, it can be useful for the web server to actually recognize the users when they are requesting a page.

There are a number of ways that cookies can be used. However they are all related to helping the website actually remember the user.

Limitations of Cookies

The majority of browsers will support cookies that reach up to approximately 4096 bytes. Due to this small amount, cookies should only be used for storing a very small amount of data, and in some cases the should be used as just an identifier. This could be the user Id which is then linked to a database that contains more information about the user.

There are also limitations imposed by browsers on the number of cookies that a website is able to keep on the user of the computer. In most cases, a total of just 20 cookies for each site can be stored. If you attempt to store additional ones, then the cookies that have an old date will be discarded. There are a number of browsers that will place a hard limit, which is typically around 300, for the total amount of cookies that they will be able to hold from all of the websites combined.

The cookie limitation may be encountered if a user has their browser set so that it does not accept cookies.

Writing Cookies in Asp.Net

The web browser being used is what is responsible for managing the cookies that are on a user's system. The cookies will be sent to a browser through object HttpResponse, which will then expose the collection referred to as cookies. This is able to be found in the property for the Response of the page class. If there are any of the cookies you wish to have to be sent to the actual browser it will have to be added in this specific collection. When you are writing a cookie, you will have to specify a Value and a Name. Each of the cookies have to have a name that is unique so that they are able to be recognized when being read from the specific browser that is being used. Since the cookies will be stored by the name, if you name two different cookies the exact same name, it will result in one being overwritten.

You also have the option to set the cookies time and date expiration. An expired cookie may wind up having the browser delete it if the user winds up visiting the website that has written the cookie. The cookie's expiration needs to be timed for a period of time that your application will consider the value of the cookie to remain valid. If you want to ensure that the cookie never expires, you should set the timing for the expiration for a period of 50 years after the date of creation.

If you fail to actually set the expiration of the cookie, then the cookie will be ready to go, but it will not be kept on the user's hard drive. The cookie will then become a portion of the visitor's session information. After the browser is closed, the cookie will also be discarded. Non-persistent cookies such as this are useful for storing information that is only needed for a short period of time.

There are a number of different ways that you can effectively add Cookies, with two examples shown here:

HttpCookie aCookie = new HttpCookie("lastvisit");

aCookie.Value = DateTime.Now.ToString();

aCookie.Expires = DateTime.Now.AddDays(1);

Response.Cookies.Add(aCookie);

Response.Cookies ["username"]. Value = "john";

Response.Cookies ["username"].Expires = DateTime.Now.AddDays(1)

These examples provide two ways to add cookies to your collection of Cookies, one that is named with username and the other that is named lastVisit.

Both of these examples will accomplish the exact same task – creating a cookie and placing it in the user's browser. In each of the methods, the value of the expiration has to be DateTime. However, with the lastVisited value there is a value for date-time. Since all of the cookies values will be stored as a string, the value of date-time will have to have a process that converts it into a String to be effective.

Cookies Containing More than a Single Value

There is the ability to store over a single value in the cookie that you create, such as the last visit and the user name. You will also be able to store several name values in pairs in just one cookie. These ae called name-value pairs, which are referred to as a subkey. These are arranged much like the

URL query string. An example of this would be to create two different cookies that are named lastVisit and username, where you have the ability to make one cookie that is called userInfo and that has the subkeys of lastVisit and userName.

You may need to use a subkey for a number of reasons. The first reason is because it can be convenient to put the similar or related information into one single cookie. Additionally, since all of the information will be in just one cookie, the attributes, including the expiration will be applied to all of the information. However, if you want to have different expiration dates to various types of information, then you need to store it in different cookies.

If you create your cookie with any subkeys it will also help to minimize the size of the cookie files. When you use just one cookie with the subkeys then you will use fewer than the limit that has been set. Also, single cookies can take approximately 50 characters total for the overhead, as well as the total length of the actual value that has been stored in it.

If you want to make a cookie that contains subkeys, you will be able to use a slight change of the actual syntax that is used for creating just one single cookie. Here are two ways that you can write the exact same cookie, with each one having two different subkeys:

```
HttpCookie aCookie = new HttpCookie("userInfo");

aCookie.Values["userName"] = "john";

aCookie.Values["lastVisit"] = DateTime.Now.ToString();

aCookie.Expires = DateTime.Now.AddDays(1);

Response.Cookies.Add(aCookie);

Response.Cookies["userInfo"]["userName"] = "patrick";
```

```
Response.Cookies["userInfo"]["lastVisit"] =
DateTime.Now.ToString();
```

```
Response.Cookies["userInfo"].Expires =
DateTime.Now.AddDays(1);
```

Controlling the Scope of Your Cookies

As a default setting all of the cookies on a particular site will
be stored with one another on the client's hard drive and the
cookies will then be sent over to your server when a request
is made to access the site. This means that all of the pages
will get the cookies that are specific to that particular
website. There are two methods you can use to set the
cookie's scope:

- Set it to a particular domain that will allow you to
  determine the subdomains that are able to access the
  cookie
- Create a limit for the cookies scope to a folder that is
  on the server.

Limiting the Cookies to an Application or a Folder

There are some cases where you may want to limit the
cookies that go to a certain folder that is on your server, but
it means that you will have to set the path properly.

```
HttpCookie appCookie = new HttpCookie("AppCookie");
appCookie.Value = "written " +
DateTime.Now.ToString();
appCookie.Expires = DateTime.Now.AddDays(1);
appCookie.Path = "/Application1";
Response.Cookies.Add(appCookie);
```

Changing the Expiration Date of the Cookies

The browser that is being used is what is responsible for the
management of the cookies. The date and time expiration set
in the cookie is going to help the browser manage the cookies

that are present. This means that you need to read the value and the name of a cookie and if you are unable to determine the expiration date and time, it should be changed.

Security and Cookies

The primary security problems that are present with cookies are very similar to those that get data from a client. In the actual web application, cookies are just another input form for users and are therefore going to be spoofing and examining. The users will be able to see what data is stored in the cookie since it is stored on their very own device. They can also change this cookie prior to the browser actually sending it back to your server.

It is important that you never store any type of sensitive data in the cookies, such as passwords, user names, credit card info or anything else. You should also not put something in a cookie that should not be accessible by a person who is trying to steal the cookie.

It is also important to be suspicious of any information that you get from the cookie. You should not just automatically assume that all of the data is exactly the same as when you created it. It is important to put in place the same safeguards when you are working with cookie values that you would with the data that users have put into a web page.

When a cookie travels from the server to the browser, it is sent in plain text. This means that anyone will be able to intercept the cookie and read what is inside of it. You can work to set the property of the cookie, which ensures it will only be transmitted if the connection is using SSL encryption. This will not protect the particular cookie from being manipulated or read while it is stored on the visitor's computer, but it will help to prevent the cookie from having someone read it while in transit.

Chapter 6: Asp.Net Goes Mobile

With a highly mobile society, ensuring your website is viewable on all the mobile devices – tablets, smartphones, etc. – is essential. For a number of web-oriented businesses and web developers this means it is more important than ever to create a quality browsing experience for any visitor who is using this type of device.

The History of Asp.Net and Mobile Browsers

The earliest versions of Asp.Net – 2.0 up to 3.5 – featured a Mobile Controls panel. This was specific server controls that were created for the various mobile devices in use. While this options is still present in the latest version of Asp.Net, it has depreciated significantly. Instead, web developers should migrate to a better and more modern approach to making their Asp.Net site mobile friendly.

The primary reason why these Mobile Controls for Asp.Net have been deemed obsolete is due to their design that is focused around the mobile devices that were around in 2005 or earlier. The markup used in these controls was cHTML or WML; however, these are no longer relevant for the majority of projects, since HTML is now considered the ubiquitous language regarding desktop and mobile browsers.

Challenges Facing Support for Current Mobile Devices

While the majority of mobile browsers will not support HTML, you will still have a challenge to overcome when you are ready to ensure your visitors have a quality browsing experience on their mobile devices:

- Bandwidth: The performance of cellular data networks can vary quite a bit and a number of the end users will be on a tariff that is charging by each megabyte used.
- Standards compliance: There are a number of mobile browsers that are not able to support the latest in JavaScript, CSS or HTML standards.
- Input methods: There are a number of devices that have keypads while others have styluses and others utilize touch. You may have to consider various navigation mechanisms, as well as additional input methods for data.
- Screen size: With mobile devices varying greatly in size and capability, the screens can often be quite smaller than the typical desktop monitor. This may result in you having to completely redesign the layout of your pages to accommodate them.

The main thing to remember is that when it comes to Asp.Net and mobile integration, there is no one-size-fits-all type of solution. The application that you create will behave and look unique according to each device that access it. Based on the mobile support level that you want, this may prove to be a more significant challenge for developers than they have ever faced in the past.

Many web developers who are considering mobile browser support for the very first time will often believe that it is only important that the latest and the most sophisticated devices are supported. The fact is, however, that there are a number of less expensive phones in use that are used on a regular basis by the owners to access the web. This means that your business will have to determine the range of devices that you want to support by thinking about who your customers are.

Architectural Options

There are three primary options for the support of mobile browsers with Asp.Net:

Solve the issue at the server. If the server is aware that it is being accessed by a device, or at minimum the characteristics of the device, it can output a different HTML markup and run a different logic. This is beneficial since it offers a large amount of flexibility and you have efficient bandwidth.

Solve the issue at the client's end. When progressive enhancement and CSS are used carefully, you will be able to create scripts, styles and markup that are able to adapt to any browser that is accessing them. This helps to render the proper "look" for the device being used and allows you to share the server side logic, but across all the different types of devices.

Device and Browser Detection

The primary prerequisite for all of the server-side techniques regarding the support of mobile devices is to know what device the visitor is going to be using. The fact is that knowing the characteristic of a specific device is more important and beneficial than knowing the model number and manufacturer. Some of the characteristics that can be beneficial include:

- The data and media formats that are supported
- The screen size in pixels and physically
- The method for input – joystick, keypad, touch, etc.
- If it is a mobile device.

It will be much more beneficial to make the decisions for mobile support based on the device characteristics, rather than model number since you will then be equipped for handling the development of future devices.

The Browser Detection Options from Asp.Net

There are a number of methods that can be used to determine the characteristics of a device. This is achieved by using the object Request.Browser. For example, you can Request.Browser.ScreenPixelsWidth or Request.Browser.IsMobileDevice, with a number of others available for use.

Even though the browser detection that is built into Asp.Net is going to be sufficient in most applications, there are two primary instances where it may not be:

- If you are trying to find out information that is more detailed regarding the capabilities of a device.
- If you want to be able to recognize the newest or latest devices.

Presenting Mobile Pages with Asp.Net

When creating the code for the server, there are a number of approaches that you can use:

- Create two different areas for mobile and desktop browsers.
- Utilize the very same controllers for the mobile and desktop browsers but ensure a different view is displayed based on the device type.
- Use the exact same controllers and the same views for each, but make the views altered with the Razor layouts.

Redirecting Mobile Users to the Mobile Location

When it comes to redirection, there are several different options to consider. A simple option is creating a filter attribute that will create the redirection if certain conditions are met:

- It is the very first request made during the session of the user
- It was initiated from a mobile browser
- Users are not requesting a resource in the actual mobile area

This filter will read: [RedirectMobileDevicesToMObileArea]

Disabling Proxy Servers and Transcovers

There are two objectives that mobile network operators have when approaching the mobile based internet:

- Ensure the number of customers who are able to share the bandwidth is maximized
- Offer the largest amount of relevant content to users

Due to the fact that most modern web pages will be designed with the larger desktop screen in mind, the connections that are used by a number of operators will use proxy servers and transcoders that can alter the displayed content drastically. In fact, they may work to modify the CSS or HTML markup in order to fit the smaller screens and they can even take images and recompress them. This can reduce the quality all for the sake of improving the delivery speed of the pages.

There is a line of code you can add to the Asp.Net form in order to ensure that the operator of the network does not mess or interfere with any of your existing code:

Response.Cache.SetNoTransforms( );

While there is no guarantee that the operators are going to take heed of this message, it is at least a start.

Mobile Page Styling for the Browser

There are a number of features and tools that will allow you to create a mobile page that you love. Keep in mind that you have to remember your end user. Consider what will be most appealing to them in order to find the right balance for your mobile pages.

You cannot ignore the mobile trend. Doing so will simply hurt your results and lead your customers straight to your competition. The good news is that with asp.net, there are a number of methods available to ensure that your website looks great no matter what size or type of device attempts to access it. Don't take a mobile site for granted, but rather take the necessary steps in order to create a user friendly site that is going to offer the needed information.

Conclusion

Thank you again for downloading this book!

I hope this book was able to help you to learn the basics of using Asp.Net. This is a relatively simple programing language to use and with a bit of practice, you will quickly become a pro.

The next step is to begin investigating some of the more advances features of Asp.Net. After all, this programming language is vast and can help you create virtually any look you desire from your website. The key is to learn to use all of the features and tools and regularly update your website to implement the latest in design techniques.

Finally, if you enjoyed this book, please take the time to share your thoughts and post a review on Amazon. It'd be greatly appreciated!

Thank you and good luck!

Are you ready to dive into the exciting world of Asp.Net? If so, finding a guide that is easy to understand is essential. You're in luck. This is exactly what you will find with this eBook. Here you can learn what the programming language is and why it is so effective. You will also learn important elements of getting started using it.

Creating a great looking website does not have to be an unreachable goal. When you take the time to learn about asp.Net and the potential it has, you will see that creating a website for your business is an obtainable and affordable goal.

Take your time, get to know the system and you will find that creating a website is something that is not only doable, but that can also be quite fun!

This eBook takes you through the proper steps and information to ensure you have a solid foundation to begin using Asp.Net. Don't sacrifice your know-how due to shoddy instruction.